Take

The Sun and the Great North Wind

Adapted by Sheila Lane and Marion Kemp

Illustrated by Joy FitzSimmons

Ward Lock Educational Co. Ltd.

Ward Lock Educational Co. Ltd.
1, Christopher Road
East Grinstead
Sussex
RH19 3BT

ISBN 0 7062 5195 4

A member of the Ling Kee Group
Hong Kong • London • New York • Singapore

Illustrated by Joy FitzSimmons
Printed in Hong Kong

 This means that the Sun is talking

 This means that the Great North Wind is talking

★ This means that you can make the sounds which go with the story.

This is the Great North Wind

This is the Sun

The Great North Wind is blowing
the clouds across the sky.

Look at me! ★
Look at me! ★
I'm the Great North Wind.
I'm stronger than anyone else in the sky. ★

Who is that hiding away up there?

Me

But **who** is it?

The Sun.
I'm the Sun.

Come out!
Tell me why you're hiding
behind that big cloud.

I'm not.

Well, I can't see you.

Look!
I'm here.

Were you hiding because you're
not as strong as me?

No.

I think you were!
You know that I'm stronger than you.

No, you're not.

Oh yes, I am.
I'm telling you Sun – I can do anything
better than you.

No, you can't.

Oh yes, I can.

Oh no, you can't.

Look how I blow! ★
I bring frost and snow.
Woo-oo-sh! ★
Woo-oo-sh! ★
Can you do that, Sun?

No, I can't do that.

The ships in the bay,
go sailing away.
Woo-oo-sh! ★
Woo-oo-sh! ★
Can you do that, Sun?

No, I can't do that.

The clouds in the sky
go flying up high.
Woo-oo-sh! ★
Woo-oo-sh! ★
Can you do that, Sun?

Yes, I can do that.

Let me see you do it then.

Go on!

Do it!

Look!

Look!

I can do it.

Well, you can't do it
as well as I can.

Yes, I can.

I'm telling you, Sun,
I can do anything
better than you.

No, you can't.

Oh yes, I can.

Oh no, you can't.

All right!
We'll have a test to see if you're
stronger than me.
Shall we do that, Sun?

Yes.

Do you see that man walking
along the road down there?

Yes, I do.

Shall we have a test to see which of us
can make him take his coat off?

Yes!
Yes!

I'll go first .....
Look at me, Sun.
Woo-oo-sh! ★
Woo-oo-sh! ★

I'm looking.

Look at me now, Sun.
Woo-oo-sh! ★
Woo-oo-sh! ★
Woo-oo-sh! ★

I'm looking.
I'm looking.

Look at me now, Sun.
I CAN make him
take his coat off.
You'll see!
Woo-oo-sh! ★
Woo-oo-sh! ★
Woo-oo-sh! ★
Woo-oo-sh! ★

See!
You can't!
You can't do it.

I give up!
I know **you** can't do it
but you'd better try.
Go on!

Look at that!

He's still got his coat on.

I can do it!

I can!

I can!

I can!

Look!

Well, well, well!
The man **has** taken his coat off.
He's put it on his arm.

Look at that!
I did it!

All right, Sun.
You win!
I think I'll go back to
my home in the sky.

Goodbye!
Goodbye, Sun!

Goodbye!

What do you think the Sun is singing
up there in the sky?